LET THE POWER WITHIN FREE YOU COMPLETELY

Let the Power within Free You Completely

Omer Dawson

iUniverse LLC
Bloomington

LET THE POWER WITHIN FREE YOU COMPLETELY

iUniverse books may be ordered through booksellers or by contacting:

iUniverse LLC
1663 Liberty Drive
Bloomington, IN 47403
www.iuniverse.com
1-800-Authors (1-800-288-4677)

Because of the dynamic nature of the Internet, any web addresses or links contained in this book may have changed since publication and may no longer be valid. The views expressed in this work are solely those of the author and do not necessarily reflect the views of the publisher, and the publisher hereby disclaims any responsibility for them.

Any people depicted in stock imagery provided by Thinkstock are models, and such images are being used for illustrative purposes only.
Certain stock imagery © Thinkstock.

ISBN: 978-1-4917-1159-0 (sc)
ISBN: 978-1-4917-1160-6 (e)

Printed in the United States of America.

iUniverse rev. date: 11/09/2013

CONTENTS

INTRODUCTION

The truth shall prevail. This is the reason for this book. Much is being done at this time, on all levels of attainment, for the betterment of mankind, and the world, as we know it. We must all rejoice in the knowledge that entities on all levels are working for the betterment of man, thus all of God's creation. We are the trusted guardians of a great trust on this plane, and we must do what we can to be made the responsible caretakers of this trust. A good place for each of us to begin, would be to keep the faith. Each soul who lives the truth, will help those about him, without even being conscious of it. Too many of us spend many lives, working hard to attain a high degree of understanding, when they need only to know that this is being done through him. Learning to live in Grace, is easier than you might think. Many think that we have been born of sin, and have no chance of ever attaining a fuller understanding of the truth.

This thought alone, can set a soul back many lifetimes. It is important for us to understand that we all have the potential of attaining higher levels of understanding, and thus being rewarded by seeing the truth and the light. The return of the Christ, nearly two thousand years ago, showed us the way this could be brought about, but through mis-interpretation, during the years, it has been made more difficult for man to understand. Now, the tide is turning, and man is searching for the truth, and is find-that salvation is (not the difficult task that some would make it.

Many of us have chosen to be here at this time, in order to help prepare the way for the coming of the Christ. Many of the souls have chosen to be near familiar souls, with sympathetic consciousnesses, that will work together in perfect harmony, for this common cause. These souls have reached a comparative level of consciousness, and are moving along the path together. The energies of these loving souls, working for the greatest good, will be able to to shatter forces of materialism, which pervades the thinking of man today. Material achievements, will in due time, be only for the greatest good of all mankind. The negative forces at work today, will have lost their power, because the bulk of all mankind will have refused to give it the power it needs to exist.

We must therefore, keep our attention focused only upon the good that is being done by the scientific community. This alone, will send an energy impulse into the scientific community, to bring about this positive goal. We must see, and acknowledge that rapid developments in science, are being done in his name, and for the benefit of all man. With this in mind, surely all swords will be turned into plow shares.

True, not all men are going to move rapidly up the path to complete freedom, because they simply are not ready for this. The mere fact that more and more souls are rising in consciousness, means that the whole of God's creation is being lifted up in consciousness. We are not to concern ourselves with the progress others are making, on this spiritual path, nor even ourselves. All we must do is realize fully, that we are loving servants of the Father. We must pick up every load, given us, and accept it as an exciting challenge, and an opportunity for us to do good, to all mankind.

If we but live in harmony with the universal law, we must rise rapidly in our spiritual understanding, and progress on the path of life. If we but become aware of the power within, we will have opened the door to greater and greater achievement. Realize the presence within, and you will see miracles happening before your eyes. Realizing this presence, only one hour on Sunday, will close the door for much good which would be coming your way. This doesn't mean that you would sit around and be concerned that you can't see these miracles taking place, as they will just be a part of your life, when you are tuned in to the Father.

This book will help you recognize the truth, when you see it. It will also help keep you from worrying where you are on this path to complete freedom. You will see, that you need not travel down the middle of the path, but you might move from side to side as you progress. The closer you remain to the center, the faster you will travel. Some of us will need those little side trips, to help fill a need in our growth, but it will not stop our progress, it will only slow it somewhat.

The material in this book will help you, if you are a jogger on this path to total freedom. God bless you, and the best to you as you make this trip.

CHAPTER I

MAKE THIS LIFE, THE ONE THAT COUNTS

You are about to open new doors that will change your life completely. Why not realize that you are of the Father, completely, and become at one with the Universal consciousness. We are about to embark upon a new journey which is taking us into strange and wonderful experiences we never thought possible. You have been building up this high point in your development for eons of time. This means that this life, then, is the culmination of many lifetimes in which you should have grown, or traveled up the path to spiritual freedom. There is reason to not believe that this is the best life ever. You may have learned much before, in a simpler life, but there is no reason you shouldn't enjoy a full, happy, satisfying, life experience this time around. For some, this may be the last time they will return to this plane, for others, it means they will progress, but that they will have to work out problems that have been left unresolved.

Some will regress this life, but they will make it up at a later date. It is much better to work out all negative aspects in your life, while you can. There is no better time than this, to make up for the mistakes of the past. As the Christ has told us, "We must be willing to drop everything, and serve the Father, who has placed us here at this time." This can mean the beginning of a loving relationship between you and your maker, which means there is no turning back. You can only surge on ahead, as you serve the Father, in an unselfish manner. Put your trust in him, and only him, completely. There can be no misgivings, or reservations. Feel this, and you are truly at one with the Father. This relationship is one that will remain with you all the days of your existence. Every moment, into eternity, will be filled with this joyous, feeling of devotion. Once this state has been achieved, you will find that you will be above the common sins which plague the average soul, who has not made this commitment.

I, and my Father, are one. This is truly the epitamy of all spiritual aspiration. Man, has for eons of time struggled to reach this state of ecstasy. Today, we find that this can better be achieved, by looking within, and this beloved union begins to take place on a higher level of consciousness than we have reached before. For this reason, this is the moment for you to make this decision, if you have not already done so. Make this decision, and you will have the hosts, on all levels, working in your behalf. This alone, will make it possible for you to move rapidly up the spiritual ladder. Never again, will you ever fear the negatives that plague many in this era of rapidly changing scenes. No more, will you ever feel alone, but you will have the blessings of the Father, in all that you do. How could one ever feel envy, when you are receiving the blessings of the Father? How could we ever want for anything, when all that he has, he has given unto us. Accept, and know these truths, and you will surely be free.

There is no better time, than the present, to make the ultimate decision, to serve the Father: hence, the reason that this life, is the one that really counts. It might be said, "How could anyone consider living as he has, up to this moment?" It doesn't make sense, that anyone would choose to feel he is struggling through life, fighting his battles all alone. The advantages for living within the Universal Law, far outweighs the reasons for living for the self. True, we can never divorce ourself from the Creator who has placed us here. He is with us always, even if we are always not fully aware of it. The faith and trust, your Father has in you, is so great; why then, can you but have a fraction of that faith in him. Once you put the teachings of the Christ first, and have but this fraction of faith; you will no longer have a need to judge your fellow man, but will feel that all those whom you meet, are truly your bretheren. You will now feel a closer relationship with all of God's creation. This feeling of closeness, with all of God's creation, will mean that you are tuning in to all creation. The law of attraction, will surely work in your behalf, if you but have this feeling about all God's handiwork. The creative God force, that binds all existence together, will, in turn, form a loving attraction to the soul who has reached this level of understanding.

We are entering an era, when all men are being asked to serve the Father, in this manner. The need is great, and the time is now, for all men to take up the banner in his name. Each one of us has a small, but important role in laying the palm branches to prepare the way for the new Christ. It is not for us to say, whether, or not, we are to pick up the banner, and lead the way, but it is for us to do. It may be difficult for some, to break out of the old lethargic habits of this era. Many, have become professional spectators at the T.V. set, but the time has come, for mankind to become an active participant in a living movement.

Why not begin at this moment to resolve to make this the beginning of an active, productive, life. Much must be accomplished in the next decade, and this is the time to begin.

This is not for us to decide, but it for us to do. Take this action, and you will have grown much, as you begin this rapid ascent to the summit. Many, who will read this, will want to know, how do they fit into this overall plan, and what must we do, to get involved? Learning to meditate, and listen for the wee, small voice, will be a beginning. Our guides, are constantly trying to come through, to give us the direction, we so desperately need. Learn to interpret your dreams, as they too, are trying to find you the direction you need. Write down the dreams, and look for the symbolism, which will tell you what you need to know. The parables that Christ used to explain the message he brought for man, is similar to the symbols used in your dreams. You are the best one to begin to interpret your dreams.

Looking within, and getting the answers from your higher-self, means that you are using this direct contact with God, through the loving teachers, and guides, who have been assigned to work with you. Your response to the teaching, which comes through you, will also help those souls who carrying out this teaching. Know these simple truths, and the truth will flow through you. Know this truth, and you will help all mankind. We are so interdependent upon souls on all levels of consciousness, who are working for the greatest good of all mankind. Never again, will you ever feel lonely, when you are alone. You will begin to cherish those moments when you are alone. Those are the moments when you will be renewing yourself for facing the exciting challenges ahead. Those periods of silence may become fewer and farther between, as you get involved in this Universal Plan. You will be so totally involved with helping your fellowman, that you will have to catch those few silent moments during the day, when you are busy, or in your sleep state. You will enjoy the silence when you are in the middle of a busy society, and will receive your direction, when you direct your attention to those moments. So few souls are willing to set their ego aside long enough to let this direction dome to come. All we must do is open the door, and let this flood of information flow through us. Let go, and let this God power work its wonders through you.

Much has been written about the proper techniques to be used in meditation, and these are helpful, but this must be something each individual must work out for himself. He, alone, must find his own way for tuning into the creative impulses of the Creator. You may use many terms for this method of receiving, but it is a personal relationship between man, and his God. It doesn't sound too difficult, but this is the most difficult thing for man to fully understand. Some, will feel that a church sect, or a personality, will have the answer for them, but they need only to look within, for the answers they so desperately need. All other souls can do, is, help bring this understanding about. The full comprehension again, is up to the individual. You may ask, "why, then, is it so difficult to fully grasp the truth, when many loving entities, from God, down, are working for my complete enlightenment?" We have so allowed the negatives to take over our thinking process, that we have allowed the dark forces to control our consciousness. Others, are so wrapped up in the material values, that fail to make room for spiritual unfoldment. These lower, thought patterns, must be controlled before you can begin to make the move toward spiritual freedom. With persistence, you will find that loving, positive, thoughts, will, more and more, become stronger and stronger. This growth can accelerate at a rapid pace, if you are persistent in the beginning, in filling your head with loving, positive thoughts which will benefit all levels of consciousness. All souls, working in our behalf, rejoice, every time we have passed a hurdle, as we move up the path. Never again, should you ever think, you are doing this, or that alone. What strength you must begin to feel, when you begin to understand the working of this law. This is why, those who follow in the truth, will seem to be so strong. This inner strength, is readily seen by those who some into contact with an enlightened soul. You need never, try to impress those about you with with your innate wisdom, or your clever use of the language. These are only the trappings of the materialistic scholar. Become spiritually involved, and you will find your place in the sun. Remain with the negative, materialistic minds, who exist in darkness, and will regress, or not show any progress up the path to complete spiritual freedom. It is hard to see, why man persists in following the later path, with no chance for advancement, when he could find complete freedom in the alternative path.

You have been placed here at this time, for a definite part in the Universal Plan. Much must be done in preparing the way for the return of the Christ. Your part in this drama can only be perceived by looking within, for the answers. Yes, your soul does know what you must accomplish during this life, but you alone must make an attempt to channel this into right action. If each one of us becomes a beacon of truth, the light will begin to light up this earth plane, which we have inherited at this time. This is an exciting challenge, and one which you may be able to fully participate in. In our Father's house, there are many mansions. It is in these mansions, that loving souls on all levels of consciousness, will be benefitting by this rapid expansion of truth and light. For this reason, it is evident that this is the time for you to fulfill your destiny on earth at this time. Now, more than ever, each of us must evolve spiritually at a faster rate than at any time in the last two thousand years.

If we fail to fulfill our destiny, we will hold back our own progress, as we can never fully understand. Much is expected of the generations born on the earth plane this century. Each of us has been preparing for this life, for eons of time. Fail in this life, and we have failed to fulfill our destiny. If we but succeed in our mission, we will have raised the consciousness of all existence in all creation.

CHAPTER II

YOUR DECISION, SHOULD
CHANGE THE EARTH

This is the beginning of a great adventure for, as you travel through the pages of this book. Let yourself enjoy the travel, as you see the picture unfold before your very eyes. You have begun to change, even as you have read the pages of this book. This change in your consciousness will affect every molecule in the picture of total existence. What a power we each possess. It may be difficult for you to understand how this could be, but, once your advance begins to become more rapid, you will see many things more clearly. The average layman, probably feels he or she has little or no influence on living matter, only a few feet from him. More and more, you will sense, and feel the great amount of energy flowing through you, either in a positive, or a negative manner. Christ was telling man that he, was of the Christ, and had the same power he possessed. Once, this sense has begun to reach your conscious mind, you have begun to expand your world from a microcosm to a macrocosmic understanding of creation.

Certainly, if you feel you will go to heaven, and spend an eternity floating around on a cloud, with nothing to do, but play a harp, this, you will surely find. If you can sense that your learning is a continuing thing, whether on this plane, or another, that you have much to accomplish to prepare for a return to the earthly plane, or to help many souls who are experiencing this physical existence, this, you will surely find true. When you begin to understand the truth, you will have an insight into the world unseen by the average senses. This extra sense, is one that comes from within. It is an inner sense that is developed only by setting aside your ego, and physical life, for one entailing spiritual understanding. This seems rather simple, it can be stated only in a few words, yet it is impossible for many to ever to achieve on this physical plane. It isn't a matter of fighting off the negative forces which attact on all sides, but, rather, it is a matter of realizing your source of power, and using that power for the greatest good of all mankind. This inner power for good, has no limitation. The only limitation would be the limitation you might attach to this power. If you say, and feel that you can only affect those about you for a distance of three feet, this will happen, but, in a negative sense, your energy has reached far beyond that point. Why not make your influence, a loving, positive one, one which will lift every molecule in existence. This is the power each of you has. This is the power you can all exert for good. This is the power of the Christ, working through you. This is the power which will prepare the way for the returning Christ.

No man will fail to see the Godliness in your makeup. You will never again be the same person you were, moments before. Just repeat the word, "GOD", several times, and you will be a different person. Repeat the word, "Love", and will again change for the better. Again, if you let hate, fear, malice, greed, and materialism, control your thinking, you will surely change, but only in a negative sense. This experience takes a long time to pull out of, or you could ask for complete forgiveness, and be freed instantly from your negative thought patterns. Yes, we can fully enjoy the many blessings the good Father has given us. These blessings may be material things about us, but you must see them as expressions of the Father. The world of negative forces, today, does give a false impression of lack on this plane. There is an abundance of energy for all to enjoy. This can only become possible, when man begins to express himself from within, from the GOD source of his inner power.

Once you begin to exist in the grace of GOD, you will find those who come in contact with you, will see this, and respond in a loving, way. Your road will be smoothed, the path will straighten out, many loving souls alongside will be aiding you on your way. Again, I keep saying, how could man fail to live only in the grace of GOD. It isn't difficult being strong, when you begin to use the power within, to work in your behalf, You need not feel that you are alone in this battle against the negative forces which bombard us on every side. These can become exciting challenges for you, as you ride smoothly over these forces in a loving, positive manner. The amount of energy which can be generated by one soul is immense. Enough energy can come from one wheat seed, to feed a nation. Think of the energy you could generate. Realize this, and you have begun to sense this energy potential within. The energy from this printed page, will begin lighting up your home, where it rests.

You need only to make the decision to serve the FATHER, in a loving, selfless way. It is your pleasure to serve him. We have been placed here at this time for a definite reason. There is a job for each of us, and who are we to question what that job might be. Some of us are destined to serve in a humble way, while others are given of the many blessings of the FATHER. From all experiences, we are learning much, or should, in any case. When we can learn the desired lessons, we begin to progress rapidly up the path to complete freedom. Some people will never begin to learn from these experiences, and they may spend an eternity working out of their static situation. Rejoice, and you will prosper, as you travel. Let the negative forces take command, and you will remain static. Who are you, to want to command, or give orders to the power within? Relax, and know that the will of GOD is being fulfilled in your life. Open the door, and let this power flow through you for good to all mankind. When you learn to embrace and love every negative force which comes into your life, you will find them as exciting challenges, which will enrich your life from this moment on. The Christ, taught us not to fear, or to resist evil, negative forces at work. When you have learned to change your consciousness, you will have complete control over the situations at all times.

Every thought you have, flowing through your conscious, or sub-conscious mind, effects even the smallest microbe, in the far reaches of creation. With this in mind, it is important to understand how important each thought is to the betterment of the universe. When you have helped even one soul to advance more rapidly up the path, you will, in turn, be helped accordingly. With practice, you will be able to help many souls during the busy periods each day, as well as during periods of rest. You too, will be able to help souls on all planes during your meditative and sleep states. These loving souls, will be helping you, as you continue on the path. This is a simplified way of describing how and why it is so important that we understand this interrelation between souls on all levels. The hierarchy, from GOD, down, is working in your behalf, if you will be willing to let it happen through you. When you can honestly feel that you alone, can do nothing, but wonderful things are happening through you; the influence you have on creation, will be greatly enhanced.

Evil, negative forces do exert a great deal of power, only when we are willing to give it that power. Usually, an evil force will destroy itself, and there will be souls on this plane, as well as higher planes, who will work for the destruction of negative force. We can refuse to acknowledge this power, and weaken it thusly. Put yourself completely in the hands of the FATHER, and you will take the sting out of negative energy. Do not concern yourself solely with those who seem to be living in a negative sphere, but do be concerned with your own spiritual advance. This will, in turn, help those who need your help. Learn to remain in tune with the Infinite energy source, and you will be immune to the effects of negative forces upon you. We know that the Christ, reached this state of consciousness, and he taught us that was we too, had this power. This simple message of the Christ, tells us that too, you can reach the Christ level of consciousness, but few have taken up the challenge.

CHAPTER III

MAKE THIS DAY COUNT IN YOUR TOTAL EXISTANCE

Begin at this moment to plan what you can do this day, which will help you become a better person. You will want to find ways of helping others, as you move about through the day. Do this, and you will be drawing forces about you which will help you in this task. Every moment devoted to negative forces, only means you have set yourself back in your forward progress by using this time thusly. Use your time in a loving, positive manner, and you will prosper as you have never before dreamed possible. This means that nothing but good, will come into your life, and you will need have no fear of dark forces which might tempt you into returning to your old ways.

Sit down at the beginning of each day, and write down three things you can do, which will help mankind forever. Begin working on these ideas today, and you may find that some things you wish to accomplish, will take more time than one day, but you have at least begun at this time. What can you do to help a soul, this day? How can you help raise the consciousness of all man? How can you help make life easier for mankind in a physical sense, and in a spiritual sense? You will begin thinking in terms of macrocosms, no longer wrapped up in your own small world, which is no larger than an atom, in the realm of all creativity. Expand your consciousness, and you begin to reach to every corner of GOD'S realm. This is such a glorious way for man to move. Remain in the Grace, and you will have no needs or wants. You will only be grateful for every moment you are experiencing on this plane. You will be moving with all creativity. You will flow with GOD'S beautiful rhythm of life.

You are about to see how important it is to think of every moment as a precious gift of the FATHER. This gift, is something you must cherish, and use to make this a better place for all. Every creature that flies, swims, or crawls on the earth will benefit by this wise use of time. Do this, and you will be recognized as a king of kings, among men. You can make good use of this time, no matter what work you have chosen to follow. The hospital orderly is in a position to help many souls, as he goes about his work. The politician, or the entertainer is in a position to help many more souls than the average person, and it is even more important for them to use their time more wisely, in his name. Think, how fast a celebrity could travel on the path, with the selfless help he could give to his fellow man. Yet, again, think how far a celebrity could regress, if he should fail to fulfill his task for good on this plane. Souls have been placed in positions to carry it off. Any soul who fails to fulfill his destiny, will surely have to come back many times to make up for his failure to do his utmost for mankind.

Yes, we all have been taught that wasted time can never be made up. It can be made up, but often it takes more time to make it up, than was wasted in the first place. Now is the time for all men to plan their lives. Begin by looking at each day, and planning that day for service to the FATHER. All that we do, must be aimed at helping the FATHER'S work, on all levels. In order to receive this instruction, you must spend more time in meditation and prayer. This reverent looking within for your instruction, will more and more, become an automatic action. Just as you do not think deliberately about every move you make in driving a car, so, too you will be taking, and following instructions from the FATHER, every moment you are on this plane. Many are making the mistake of giving orders to the FATHER; telling what they need, and giving him many tasks to perform, every day. How much better it would be, if we could ask the FATHER to steer our ship of state, and we would be the loving servants who would do the rowing. This guidance, is what we need, to make the most of every moment, every day. You will find that many souls will be sent your way, only to help make your work even easier. For this reason, it is important to become fully involved with life, as we know it. Those, who strictly follow some Eastern philosophies, by selfishly sitting in meditation day after day, year after year, and do not contribute to helping mankind, rather than taking from others, will not move up the path as rapidly as those who are involved with GOD'S plan.

As man begins to use his time, in His name, more and more, will the Universal Plan unfold. The small germ will grow at such a rapid pace that the earth will rejoice as one, in his name. Many prophecies of doom, showing the power of the dark forces, will be vanquished before our very eyes. Sickness, misery, and poverty, will all be a thing of the past. We will begin to see the brotherhood of man emerge as a powerful force for good. The answer for us in living in GOD'S Grace, is so rewarding, it is difficult to see how some can cling to the old thoughts that have filled men's minds, since the beginning of time. It may seem impossible for this ideology to take hold, but the smallest seed can make this possible. Know that GOD is in his holy temple, and all is right with the world. All is being done in his name. All material developments that surround us will suddenly become the work of the FATHER. When man begins to see the GOD-power within all material possessions he may enjoy, he will no longer be worshipping false idols. Man will suddenly enjoy all of GOD'S many blessings which have been bestowed upon him. Man will sense this tremendous energy of the CREATOR, all about him, in making up his total environment.

St Francis was one who attracted all of GOD'S living creatures to him in a loving way. You too, will be attracting all of GOD'S abundance, and creation to you, in a loving way. You will thoroughly enjoy all the blessings of the Father, but will, in no way, try to possess them. You will no longer need to possess for the sake of possessing, but will be able to use GOD'S abundance in carrying out the task set before you. All GOD'S creation will be working with you for your continued success, as you work within the Universal Laws. Understand this precept, and you will have the wisdom that has taken eons of time to evolve. You will know that GOD is all there is, there is nothing else. Once you have begun to understand this concept, you will be able to visualize the existence of GOD, as he exists on all planes. Know these things, and you will never again fail to feel your oneness with the Father. How could you ever again be separated from the Father? Every aspect of GOD'S creation will respond in a positive manner to your loving appreciation of it. Be still, and know that I am GOD. The I, is all inclusive of divine creation.

You are now able to understand why so many great souls have been able to accomplish so much, during a lifetime. This very law, one which consists of using your time wisely, is the secret of rapid growth in the spiritual realm. Some souls are content to spend most of their earthly existences, wasting their time in a frivolous manner. This waste can be made up, only by diligent endeavor on the part of the erring soul. Stay in the good Grace of the Father, and you will undoubtedly be using your time in a constructive manner; one which is helping fulfill your destiny in completing the Universal Plan.

Now, many are going to say that they have no conception of their role in this plan. This may be so, if you are not attempting to stay tuned in to the Universal Power. The task is made easy for us, as we have opportunities for learning, thrust at us every day. We also have many tests and challenges which confront us, as we move through each day. How we respond, and react to these challenges, determines how we have evolved, and how the Universal Law works through us. We are constantly meeting souls who have been placed in our midst, merely to help us on our way. Some will help, by offering challenges, which are learning situations for our greatest good. We may not feel that those souls were here to help us, but your own reaction to those situations, will determine whether or not you have been helped by them. Nothing is left to chance. It is all a part of a beautiful plan, and we are the actors involved in the production of this life scene. With the proper understanding, you will begin to grow at a rapid rate, as you continue up the path. Place yourself in the loving hands of the Father, and you will flow easily through all existences. Your complete faith will sustain you, in all you will encounter.

Since we are all actors in this Universal production, we cannot succeed if we do not recognize our director. It is up to us to come across as well as we might, but we must always look to the director for our directions. Some make the sad mistake of feeling they are self-made actors, and that no direction is needed where they are concerned. No man is an island unto himself, but, rather, he is interdependent upon all creation for his existence.

This direction, is such that we must be attuned to it every moment of every day. No longer will the Sabbath be holy, but every moment of every day will become holy in our eyes. Once man has begun to understand this concept of living, he will begin to make every moment count in his total existence. Even in moments of rest and relaxation, you will find this time devoted to the working of the Universal Plan. This time too, can be useful to generate more power for your part in the next scene. Proper prayer and meditation, will be a time for you to receive direction from the Father. It is up to us, as free souls, to open our consciousness to the Father, who has placed us here for a definite purpose. All we must do, is set aside our personal ego, which closes the gate to this understanding. Set your ego aside, and you will be free to accept the Universal Knowledge, from the Masters on all planes. Once you have begun to become a channel, such as this, you will indeed be blessed in the sight of those Masters. This concept can make you a channel for good, on this plane.

CHAPTER IV

YOU ARE ONE WHO IS ON THE WAY OF THE TRUTH

How have you come this far, and what must you do to stay on the path? It is only natural to wish to understand why we are here at this time. We have gathered here at this time to be among other familiar souls who have traveled similar paths. We are working with other souls to help carry out the Universal Plan. Certainly, some of us will be able to remain steadfast, on the path. Those of us who are fortunate enough to understand what it is that we must accomplish, during this lifetime, will be able to help others realize their purpose for this life. Your sub-conscious mind, does know why you are here, and what it is that you must accomplish. Your conscious mind may not have the slightest idea the why, or wherefore of our being here at this time. It may be difficult for us to understand this path of the truth. Yes, we are all on this path, but there are many levels of attainment, as we move along that path. This path does lead the way to the truth.

For some, it might be difficult to understand why some souls we may come in contact with, could conceivably be on a path of truth. When we begin to doubt, or question this purpose for all man, we begin to set ourselves up as being a little better than other souls, and then determine that their path is one to destruction, and hell. Certainly, some may regress for a short time, others may not show much progress during a lifetime, but they are surely on the path to truth. Understand this concept, and you will see your fellow-man in a new light. It will be easy for you to see the divinity of all man.

We have all been used to people doing things which we may or may not understand. How and why these behavior patterns develop, is something which is set before the soul returns to this plane. Many souls have had such varied experiences with those with whom they come in contact with, they will behave in a manner according to this previous background. Those who react in a negative manner to those who may have wronged them in a previous life, will find that they have either slowed their progress up the path, or they may have regressed to a point which would take many lifetimes to make up. Be this as it may, it is important to react in the Christ-like manner which is expected of us, when we are confronted with these forces as we travel. If one is able to meet these problems and solve them in a Christ-like manner, he will begin to move rapidly up the path to complete freedom.

We all have much to learn. This is why we are here at this time and place. This is a final proving ground for many who are moving at a rapid pace up the path. Others are preparing themselves for other lives which give them opportunities to advance rapidly. You may wish to ask why nothing is said about the methods of achieving a more rapid movement up the path. The basic truths which are given in the Bible, are the foundation for such a rapid movement. Every soul who is helped by you, gives a big impetuous to your spiritual growth. Help one soul move more rapidly up the path, and you will be rewarded in a like manner. Every spoken word, every thought, and every action is being added to your record of achievement. Make every action a loving positive one that will count for something in your relationships with all souls.

No man could go wrong with this attitude. Certainly you must love others as you do yourself, and you must surely love yourself if you are to progress rapidly. Many souls are holding back their foreward progress, only because they are finding fault and chastising themselves, either to themselves or in the presence of others. This negative reaction toward oneself is a direct way of blinding oneself to the truth. You are as important to the success of God's plan for the Universe as anyone, or anything that has been created by the Father. God is all in all. There is nothing else. All is spirit. Know this, and you will be free.

Others will progress rapidly, only because they will tune in and remain tuned in to this creative spirit, every moment of their earthly lives. Now, how can I do this when I must work at a job, or do the menial chores required of me? Once you have learned the method of remaining in touch with the infinite, you will ask yourself, "Why did I not do this before?" This oneness with the creative spirit, will of itself make this all possible. This attitude will become an automatic reflex which opens all doors, and smooths the path before you. It becomes difficult for those who pile up the negatives in their path, and make all the extra work for themselves. Who would wish to build a freeway with the obstacles in its path that the average man places before himself.? You can be free of these challenges instantly. You can smooth the path before you instantly. Accept it, know it, and believe in it completely. Have the faith of the little child. Know these things, and you are made free. Reject these truths, and you will continue climbing over the obstacles you have placed there.

Man who has attained this level, and begins a rapid ascent up the path, is said to inherit the earth. Your physical appearance has nothing to do with your advancement as a loving soul of the Father. Man's color, size, sex, or status in life, have nothing to do with spiritual progress as such. These physical differences do mean that they are aspects he has chosen to endure, which will help overcome previous Karma which had limited his spiritual progress. A handsome, soul who uses this to bring others farther up the path, will surely prosper, but he that will misuse this trait will suffer from his actions. Often these traits offer a soul an opportunity of rapid spiritual advancement, only because they had misused their more advantageous attributes in previous lives. When you know that every aspect of your being is divinely created, you will no longer find fault with your physical attributes. Be thankful for the way you are. Experience this fullness of the Father within, and you will have to tell no man. Every soul you meet will know this to be true.

This book is not meant for those who live in white houses, or those who drive a particular car, nor is it just for those who have married and have children. It is not just for those who attend church, but it is for all mankind. All mankind is on the path to truth. It is not up to you or I to judge the actions of other souls on this path. Yes, some may be slipping, but have you never slipped? Some will not react as you would have in certain instances, but that does not make the better for it. Let the Father be the judge, and you will be a loving, helping soul. Look for the good in your fellow-man.

Now you have begun to know and feel the matter in which the true Christian soul is traveling up the path, or how he should be traveling along the path. Yes, you have become enlightened to a certain degree about these truths, but you must now open your hearts to these truths, and make them an everyday existence in your lives. Learning to live, and travel in the light, is the aspiration of all mankind. This aspiration is easier to follow than most are led to believe. Sure, there are pitfalls along the way, but you will surely succeed in moving rapidly up the path if you will but still your attention only upon the FATHER. Make him a part of every moment in your lives, and you will surely be rewarded.

God is in his holy temple. You will now ask, "Where is that holy temple"? That temple is within yourself. It is part of your inner consciousness. It is that part of you which is inevitably tied to the FATHER with a golden cord. We are all puppets, so to speak. We all have the free choice to make decisions, whether they be right or wrong, but we are still connected the creative force that has placed us here. This connection remains with us always, whether we realize it or not. The FATHER is with us always, no matter how far we may stray. This is why it so easy for us to get back on the path. Once you have truly renounced your sins, you can never go back as you were before. Sure, you may slip from time to time, but you will still be advancing up the path. The most rapid growth of course, is made by those who can keep their eyes set only on the FATHER, and live completely in the truth.

We do have the option of traveling at a rapid pace, or making little or no progress at all, or even regressing somewhat. This is a decision for us to make. Do his bidding, and you live in peace.

CHAPTER V

MAKE THIS MOMENT ONE YOU WILL REMEMBER

This is the most important moment of your life. This is the moment that counts. This alone, is the sum total you will experience during this life. You live in the present moment, only in that moment. The burdens and errors of the past, have nothing to do with the present. They need not affect it in any way. The uncertainty and fears of the future, should have no effect on the present. These do, in essence affect the present, and how much we can enjoy the moment. You will surely enjoy each moment if you can place yourself completely in the hands of the FATHER of us all.

We have much to be thankful for. If we can fill many of our present moments being thankful for the many blessings which we enjoy, we will have little time left for the little negatives that may sneak in concerning the past or the future. If you do not regularly give thanks, you may wonder what you can be thankful for. This very suggestion, may seem absurd for those who are forever grateful, but for those who are not, the following will help you understand. First, when you are being grateful, you are giving thanks for God's many blessings bestowed upon us. You may be grateful for the air you breathe. Without this life-sustaining force, you could not exist. You may be grateful for being. This is something we all take for granted, but it is through a miracle that you have been made manifest into a physical body. You may be grateful for the perfect health you enjoy, or the perfect understanding which will manifest perfect health in your body. You may give thanks for the many friends you have, because they have all been brought to you for a purpose. Be grateful for the many obstacles in your life, as they are exciting challenges for you to meet.

This list of things to be grateful for can grow and grow, Each of you will wish to be grateful for different things. You will all place different priorities on these items to be grateful for. Some will place food, or other material values on items to be grateful for, while others will concentrate on more spiritual blessings.

You will choose your blessings for which you are grateful, according to your position on the spiritual path. No two souls are the same. You might say, "Thank God", and you will surely be correct in this assumption. What you choose to be grateful for, will be right for you, at this moment. Another moment, or another time, and you will feel a need to be grateful for something else. The important thing to remember is, be grateful. When you learn to give thanks for your blessings, you open doors that have previously been closed to you. You have begun to advance more rapidly on the path, as you no longer have time for the negative thought that filled your mind, before. Before you know it, your whole concept of God has been changed, without your even knowing why. Be grateful every moment, and you will be free. You can receive no greater joy, than giving thanks to the FATHER, for his bountiful blessings.

Now, that you have learned to free yourself to enjoy every moment as you experience it, you will need to understand in a larger sense, the complete joy of the moment. Let the Power, and the strength of the FATHER, flow through your complete being, through and through. Revel in the ecstasy of this feeling of at-oneness with GOD. You are a part of the whole, and the whole has its being in you.

Be that as it may, you have come upon a basic truth which makes you different from other souls on this plane. This moment is a moment completely different from the previous moment you have just experienced. Are you happy with the moments you have just completed? If not, you may begin at this moment making the most of every moment in your life. You may now begin to wonder how or what this might be. How do I get the most from every moment? These are constantly being asked by souls, but few ever do anything constructive about this matter, which will help them move more rapidly along the path.

You may begin by sitting down and analyzing just what you have accomplished in the last few moments. Write them down in a tablet. Then go back during the day, and ask yourself just what you have accomplished constructively, then do this with the previous day, week, month, and year. If you have listed your positive achievements, you will begin to see a pattern evolve which shows the course you should be following. If you have many negative elements entering into your past, you will want to look at yourself objectively, and see how you can place this wasted energy into productive action from now on. You have begun this change, the moment you decided to look back and see yourself. You may now list the positive things you have accomplished, and will want to add to this list in the future. "How can I go about this?" You may ask. If you will but sit in quiet meditation, you may tune yourself in to the divine Christ center of your being. Here, you will receive answers to your questions. Learn to sit quietly in his presence, and you will know. Maybe you will hear a voice, or will just be able to jot down the answers in a tablet. Reevaluate your objectives from time to time, as your needs will change as you travel. How much more you will receive from every moment on this plane.

This does not mean that you must be active every moment, it means that you must have a balance between an active, constructive life, and getting yourself tuned in and recharged with energy periodically during the course of the day. Your physical body is not a perpetual motion machine, and if you love yourself as you should, you will find that you will need to let down completely. Meditation techniques are important to achieve this rest effectively, during the day. Learning to recharge yourself will give you the energy to accomplish the course of action you have outlined for yourself. Every moment will be more effective with this balance. Both, are charged with energy, one is in the physical, and the other is in the spiritual realm. The more complete this balance, the more in-tune with the FATHER, you will become. You are now beginning to let the FATHER within, do the works. You will now begin to realize that it isn't you but he that doeth these works. Believe this, and you have everything in its right perspective. Do this, and miracles of accomplishment will begin taking place in your lives.

Learning to use the power and the strength of the FATHER, flowing through you, and you will be renewed in his strength to accomplish all that you must do in his name. You do not have to think, I must be humble, through all of this. You will be humble. It is as simple as that. You need not go through life always trying to do the work of the Lord. Relax, and let him work through you for his greatest good. You are truly his instrument for good. Let this happen, and every moment will be a sacred moment with the FATHER, working through you. He knows why you are here at this time, and your higher self also knows why, but it is only a matter of your tuning in to learn to put all this to work in a conscious manner. Be still, and know.

Now that you have the plan, you will need to know how you will benefit from all this. What do you get out of all this. This is what we are all interested, in this materialistic society. Do his bidding, and you never want for anything. The kingdom is yours. The FATHER, knows what your needs are, you do not need to keep reminding him of the various things you need. Do his bidding, and your prayers will be answered. You need not wonder how, or why, but that the prayers will always be answered if you have but the faith of a grain of mustard seed. When you begin to live in his Grace every moment of your life, you can expect miracles in every facet of your existence.

This moment is important because it is the sum total of all existence for you, including the past and the future. It is no wonder why every moment is so important to each of us as we travel. Fill each moment full of loving, giving thoughts, and you will receive the same from the FATHER, all this, and more. Only GOD, as your true employer, can make a deal like this for you. Why don't more people take advantage of a situation like this? Most can't believe all this can be true. It is too good to be true. Yes, it is, but this is the way GOD works through us. There need never be any fear of anyone or anything, when you have reached this level of consciousness. Only the greatest good coming from the FATHER, can be expected in your life. From this moment on into eternity, you can be a soul who can and will be the Christ-like disciple on this earth plane. Others will look to you for guidance, only one in your capacity would be able to offer. Yesterday you may have nothing to offer, and today, you are a perfect Christ-like disciple working in his behalf. This is an altered state of consciousness, one in which you can be transformed in an instant. This is part of the simple message Christ gave us, but many are reluctant to accept this challenge. Every day more and more are accepting this challenge, and this is the wonder of it all.

This is probably more than many can accept, but it is such a simple truth that it can easily be bipassed, for other doctrines which sound much more intellectual. Man often is challenged, not by simple facts, but by complicated theories concerning those facts. Christ was the ideal teacher, because he cut through the garbage, and came up with the simple truths needed to follow in the path of the FATHER. Those very same loving, giving thoughts that are given off from more and more souls, are having a positive effect on the world, if not the universe. It is becoming increasingly more difficult for those who continue living outside GOD'S realm, so to speak. These loving, positive vibrations are engulfing the whole of the universe. The minute one soul begins to raise himself in consciousness, he will in turn, raise the consciousness of the whole world. The elevated thought of this moment will elevate the thoughts of man for all time. You are important in the working of GOD'S plan, as only you will know. This is why every moment is so important in the working of GOD'S plan. Every moment in your life must be a loving, giving moment, one in which the greatest good is being manifested through you for all mankind.

It is important that you do not concern yourself with the negatives you see around you every day. You do not have to resist them, or fight them, you need only to live in grace and flow with them. These negatives will have little, or no power, if you do not give them power. Accept the fact that many souls you will meet have not even started on the path, while others may be on this path, but not where you are. You can never look at another, and think that he may not be on the path, or that he might be lower than you you on this path, you must only realize that he too is a child of the FATHER, as you are. Observe others about you in this manner, and you have helped them, as well as helping yourself move up the path.

You have often heard that the path narrows, near the end, and this is true, only because you have learned to focus your attention only on the FATHER. Nothing else will matter at this point in your advancement. Nothing can deter you from your advancement at this point. At some time in your development, you will recognize this truth. Believe as a little child, and you will be invincible. All mankind will eventually realize that God is all there is, there is none other. All creation has been manifest in his name. Many cannot conceive how completely free they will be if only they could visualize this realization with the creative energy pervading all matter on this plane.

CHAPTER VI

TAKE THE TRUTH TO THE WORLD

This might sound a little far-fetched in this time, as mankind is so preoccupied in just making a living, paying taxes, and meeting the many obligations which come along. Yes we have problems which must be surmounted, but so did people at the time of Christ have many of these same problems. Christ left his work to administer to the needs of mankind. He was here to help mankind grow spiritually, but he also alleviated them of hunger and disease. If you are to administer to the spiritual needs of mankind, you must first, speak to them at the level they will understand. Do not try to convert souls into believing the theory of reincarnation, when they are not ready for this.

You will soon begin to realize that you will do much more for mankind when you can fill his spiritual needs at his level. This level will be easy for you to discern, when you will let the FATHER, flow through you. You will never need to concern yourself about expressing yourself to those people, if you will remain tuned in to your divine source. The longer you continue to do this, the easier it will be for the FATHER to express himself through you. Realize you are the instrument, and these miracles will begin to happen through you. If you will never take the credit for these miracles, you will leave the channel open, so they may continue to flow through you, for the good of all mankind. Do this, and you will continue rising up the spiritual path at a rapid rate. You are being benefitted in direct proportion to the help you give to others on this path.

"How do I take the truth to the world?" you might say.

All mankind will be doing this in a different manner. Some will feel a need to preach to the masses, while others will wish to be the perfect example of one who has attained a high level of consciousness. You are on stage, every minute. Your audience is all around you. You are also being monitored by higher souls on other planes. Nothing is left out of your actions, or your thinking. You really fool no one, your actions will be understood by the higher selves of those with whom you are coming in contact. Others may or may not be reading you directly, but sooner or later, they will see you as an open book. Others will soon see the Christ like quality in your being, without your even trying to be this way. Others will notice when you have been elevated in consciousness. You will never need to try to impress anyone with your perfect bearing, as this will be quite obvious. When you become aware of your actions, and try deliberately to impress others with your innate goodness, you will surely fail in fooling anyone. Be ye humble in the eyes of the Lord, and your will have the power of kings.

You need not recount all the good things you are doing for others, as this is recorded in the acashic records. Every loving, positive, action you give in the relationships with others; will help raise the spiritual level of all mankind. Every loving thought sent out by you, will be returned many, many times to the you, the sender. The positive benefits to be derived from living a loving,

Christian life, are so great, that you may wonder why man has chosen the path of darkness.

The rewards are so great, for living a Christ-like life, yet many continue living in the darkness through ignorance. It is up to you to spread the light all over this planet. You spread the light every time you help another along the path. You also dim the light, when you live through ignorance of the truth. How much better it would be if we continued to live in truth, and spread the light. Through the quiet moments of meditation, you will intuitively know what course of action you must take. You will be able to do this in many ways right where you are. You need not depend on anyone but yourself. You can never blame others because you have failed to be as effective as you might have been. This is only possible, when you can tune in, and take your orders from your higher self. Each of us has a course of action he must take, and never ask why? You are committed to fulfilling the divine plan. Once you committed yourself to a course of action, you must never turn back, or falter.

There are many facts to the truth that you must teach. The average laymen on the street may not understand the truths that a high level soul understands. Teach only the truth, as sees fit for the moment. Do not tell all the truths you have come to understand, to all mankind. Yes, you meet great teachers, and will be able to discuss all truths with them. You will be able to teach these many truths in your sleep state to many who are ready for it. You will be able to teach many merely by your presence. The charisma of the Christ is almost powerful force. Use this, and all man will benefit for all time.

This Christ presence is what is needed to make the divine plan work for the greatest good of all mankind. Since we are all the sum total of all our experiences, we all have something different to add to the success of the divine plan. We all have been placed here at this time for a definite purpose. Each of us may be only a small part of the total working for the advancement of all men up the spiritual ladder. Yes, we are all unique, but vitally important in carrying out the work set before us.

Your higher self knows what your part in this plan is to be, and the best way to find these answers is in meditation, "looking within", for your purpose. Once you have become aware of your purpose in life, you must strive to bring this about. Let no man deter you from completing your mission. If you leave yourself open to temptation, you will spend much valuable time in continuing on making up for this lost time. Once you have dedicated yourself to serving the FATHER, you must never turn back. You must fulfill your destiny, for which you spent eons to time preparing for. You will attract those around you who can help you in fulfilling your destiny, and situations will arise which will give you the opportunity to bring this about. You are continually being tested and evaluated, and how you respond to this testing, determines exactly how and how fast you will be ascending up the path.

Nothing is left to chance. You must learn to respond to situations placed before you in a loving, positive way. If, for any reason you will fail in any portion of this test, you must immediately sit down and evaluate the problem, and correct your response as it should have been. You will soon begin to see that more and more your responses will automatically become those loving, positive ones which you have been striving for. You will no longer have to think about how you should react to a certain situation, as you will automatically do the correct thing. This is truly the Christ, as he works through for all mankind. Crowd your thinking with these loving-positive thoughts, and only keep your eye centered on the source of all truth, and you will have no time left for the negative, dark side of life. You will not have to fight evil, you will have won by your overwhelming desire to live the truth as it should be.

Souls of like consciousness are drawn together to work in his behalf. Other groups are working on different levels, either, or lower than your own, but each in his own way is working for the greatest glory to the FATHER. Some souls have shown great spiritual growth when they have been involved in a negative experience, such as a war; while others have become animals in such situations. During a period of strife, you must carry only loving thoughts for all who are involved in the conflict. Who are we to take sides when we are all brothers, created in his name. Know this truth, and you will no longer feel that you are superior to any man. You will only know that you are his brother, and that you have the same FATHER. It has taken us so long to learn this. We have had the greatest teachers during the ages, but have not heeded the truth.

The time will come, when all men know the truth, and will live it without giving any thought to the dark forces. When this happens, men will be free to travel anywhere on this planet without a passport. There will be no race consciousness, or allegiance to any country. There will be only our allegiance to the FATHER who has placed us here to do his work. Every soul who lovingly follows in the path of truth, will help bring about the day when all men will surely be working in divine order. We all live in a world of material forms created by our heavenly Father, which must work in complete divine order in order to exist. How long would a man or beast exist if they did not exist in perfect divine order? A tree could not exist if all its component parts did not work together in divine order. Change the molecular structure of stone, and it no longer remains the same. Divine beauty surrounds us, know this, and you begin to see the beauty of divine creation all about you. We are all part of the whole. Yes, it may be only a small insignificant part of that whole, but that little bit is responsible for the working of the divine plan; just as a small cell in the human organism is important to the working of the complete whole being. There is a void which cannot be filled if we fail to fulfill our destiny, as servants of the FATHER. This is the very reason you will find weak areas in the successful application of the divine plan. As each soul begins to live the truth, he influences others about him to do the same, until all souls have begun to live on a higher level than they did before.

No matter how we try, we can never divorce ourselves completely from the creative force which has placed us here. No matter how hard we try to separate ourselves from this force, we are again faced with with it every time we take a breath of air. We must continually use the same air as does all animal life, in order to exist.

We have all become used to this force, but have failed completely, to realize the true meaning of this common force flowing through us all.

How could one ever feel superior to another, with this simple understanding of the truth. We have but to realize this, and we begin to realize how this common bond between all life, helps unite us all with the creator. We will never be able to separate ourselves from the creator, but we can put this knowledge of divine order in the back of our heads, only to keep cropping up time and time again to haunt us. We are at one with this divine order, or we would cease to exist on this plane. Know this truth, and you will be able to carry this message to the world.

The truth does exist in all creation, but we must look for it, if we have not been made aware of it before. You are all emissaries of this truth to all mankind. You need not meet all souls in person, but will be able to help others in meditation, sleep state, or in your waking state. The later is one of a limiting nature, but the personal contact can be very effective in teaching the truth. Entertainers, artists, world leaders, etc. are able to reach many people with the modern media which can carry their message to a greater number of people. This can either help them to grow spiritually at a rapid rate, or they may retard their spiritual growth for eons to come; dependent upon the positive or negative aspects of their actions.

We must remain in the mainstream of living, in order to achieve this goal set for us. You cannot become a monk in a far off monastery, and influence the greatest number of people on this physical level. You can in some respects, reach others in a meditative or sleep state, but the effectiveness of this depends upon the spiritual heights you may have reached. Even Christ, found it important to work directly with the disciples in this physical plane. The disciples, in turn, found it important to have this physical contact with the masses, in order to spread the word. Again I say, it is not important to speak in order to get the message across. The light and energy given off by a true disciple, will be enough to light the world with the truth. Again, you must never try to impress another with your vast knowledge, or prowess, but know that this message to all man is flowing through you. We are all instruments for either good or evil. If there is good, then there must be evil. There need not be either of the two previous statements, if you will but acknowledge the truth of your being. You must know your purpose in life, and fulfill this to the best of your ability. This need not be difficult if you will recognize the true source of your strength. If you feel sorry for yourself, you will only lack the energy to accomplish the task set before you. GOD will not take, "NO", for an answer. He doesn't understand what it is to tire, as he has an endless amount of energy to bestow upon you. Do these things, and you will surely be a King of Kings, among the men on this earth.

CHAPTER VII

DO THIS, AND YOU WILL REJOICE IN THE TRUTH

Introduction;

It is time for you to understand why the truth is hard for the non-believer to comprehend. This is a study about the reason for men becoming involved in the fulfilling of God's plan for him. It is not for us to question, but only for us to act upon. Understand this, and you will begin to know the truth. Knowing the truth makes it possible for you to act upon this knowledge. This truth is within every soul on all places, but few are able to conceive of this. Open your eyes, and let the truth be known to all men. You are among those who have become aware of this. The mere fact that you are becoming involved with this truth, helps you to understand the meaning of this truth. Truth is such a simple thing; it is only that man has tried to cover the truth with a myriad of facets which conceal its true identity. True revelation is such a simple thing. It is something which happens only to those who let themselves become receptive to the truth. It is here, and it has been here all the time.

Some of us have been blinded by our own selfishness, and our egos, which tend to block out the truth from our eyesight. Know the reason for your existence, and you will know the truth. You can get the proper perspective, merely by sitting quietly and knowing the Father within who knows all things. It is not for you to seek the truth, the truth is there for all to see. This chapter will be concerned with those who desire to know the truth, but are unsure of the correct way in which to search for it. You do know that certain materials will react in a definite way when certain changes take place in the physical environment. So, too, you will be able to understand what changes are taking place within your own higher self, which will open the doors and let you see the truth and the light. You may even think that this is not for me, but for other souls who are either more worthy of this, or this are more ready for this acceptance.

Jesus brought us a simple message, but man has covered this basic truth with a myriad of camouflages and diversions which confuse this truth. Know that you are a true servant of the Father, and you will be able to focus your attention only upon the truth and the light. Think that you alone can act in the completion of your duties, and you will fail to be aware of the truth. You do not need a book to tell you of these truths, you need only that God alone is in charge of your destiny.

This is the time to rededicate yourselves to the search for this truth. Truth is always available, yes, it is at your fingertips, but seldom do we realize this, as we continue along life's path. Be still, and know that this knowledge is within your own consciousness, if you would but look within for this. Yes, we can forsake our Father, and never be aware of his presence, but this does not mean that you have been forgotten by the Father in heaven. He is with you always, and you will be reaping the benefits of his presence, even without this knowledge on a conscious level. Know this, and you will never again feel alone, but will always feel that you are being helped in many ways by the creative power of the Father. How else could you ever again fail in any accomplishment you would set out to accomplish. You will become an invincible servant of the Lord, going about doing his bidding. If you fail to heed this challenge, you will find a veil has covered the truth as you should see it. It is there for all to see, but few who pass this way, will ever be aware of its presence. Follow in the footsteps of our loving Lord, and you will surely see the light, and know the truth. If you continue to alter your course, you will surely walk in darkness.

Your light beam will meet with that of many other loving souls whose lights shine as does yours. This coming together of many souls will benefit all mankind, as much good will be accomplished in his name. This is all being orchestrated on higher levels, and we are but the instruments by which this is all being manifest on this level, at this time.

How then could we but realize our oneness with this creative energy of our loving Father. The basic truth that the Christ brought to man is such a simple thing. We have incorporated much dogma, and pomp in the carrying out of this teaching. We have begun to worship the material values of the church, which have become idolic worship which again hides the truth from us. Recognize your small part in the makeup of the whole divine plan, and you will begin to sense this truth as it manifests itself before your eyes.

Let yourself be an instrument for good on this plane. Know that you can do nothing, but all good is being accomplished through you. You need not consciously put effort into the doing it yourself, but only need to be aware that this is all being accomplished through you. You do not need a gold star for every good deed you may accomplish, you need only rejoice at the privilege of being able to do these things in his name. Your ego is God's ego. Why should you try to get credit for every good thing you might accomplish? Even when your fellowman begins to pat you on the back, you may not take the credit. Always give credit where credit is due. No man is worthy of this. If you insist upon taking credit for all good things that you think you are doing, you are playing God. You may be of the Father, but you are not God!

If you can but begin to understand your rightful place in God's scheme, you will be able to see the veil fall away, and the truth will shine through. There will no longer be any reason for any of us living in the darkness, but we can become shining beacons of light. If we will but carry the torch for our Father, we will begin to crowd out the darkness around us. Negative forces will cease having any power as they are confronted by the forces carrying the light of the Father. If you resist the dark forces, you will fail. Become a beacon of light, and all darkness will melt away before you. If one loving soul would stand for but one candlepower, think of the tremendous power generated by millions of souls. Light attracts more light, as they meld together to raise the consciousness of all mankind. When this day comes, all hosts on all levels will rejoice.

This force for good is contagious, as light attracts more light. There is no room for those who half heartedly will follow in the footsteps of our loving Christ Jesus. If you have made a commitment to serve him in his name, you must be willing to follow this to the letter. There is no room for those of faint heart, as those thus involved, will be strengthened as others will never understand. You will have much help in achieving your goal as you will be aided by souls on all levels, who are working in your behalf. Forget the idea that you must walk on this narrow path by yourself, but realize that God, and all his creation is helping keep you on that path. Know this, and it will be much easier for you. You can do your part, by letting the light shine forth at all times. This is accomplished by realizing your source and your purpose for being at this time and place. This could never happen if you make no commitment on your part. Once you have committed yourself to serving the Christ, you will have this help on all levels, but you must first make this commitment.

Once you have begun to acknowledge this fact, you will begin to arrive at a place where souls have worked to achieve. This is the culmination of work and planning for eons of time necessary to make this ultimate step. Man has always felt the separateness from God. This occurred with the advent of Adam partaking of the apple in the Garden of Eden. Recognize your kinship with the Father, and you will have arrived at the place of the most high. This is where souls of high development have arrived, and have their being. This is above the emotional level achieved by most souls on this earth plane. Once you recognize this kinship, you will achieve goals you never dreamed possible. You will begin to understand why loving souls have been drawn to you in this life. They all have some part in your training. You have much to learn from these souls. They may be on other levels of consciousness than yours, and this is good. You will be able to help others rise in consciousness, and others in turn will be able to help you advance also. You have much to learn from these encounters, and how you react toward these souls depends upon your being to learn from these encounters in either a positive or negative way. Every soul, no matter how insignificant, has a reason for meeting with you at this time and place. You are being monitored on higher levels for your response to these experiences. This is being done in a loving, positive manner. It is not meant to throw the fear of God into you for every misstep you might take. The important thing is to learn from your mistakes, and be able to advance that much faster up the path. It is those who do not not learn from their mistakes that only regress during this life cycle.

This is the option we all have as we move along the path to complete freedom. There is nothing to gain by making wrong decisions, but only the greatest good comes out of the right decisions made by man. Some, through Karmic mistakes, feel they must suffer the tortures of the dark forces as they travel this way. The loving Christ said that man could be completely forgiven of his sins in a moment, and would never have to return to them. Still we have those who feel they must torture themselves in order to achieve complete redemption. How could man but fail to see the advantages of living the good life as Christ has shown us? If you would but learn to live the truth, you would make such rapid strides up the path during this life, you would find no reason for ever returning, unless it was of your own volition to serve mankind.

Yes, we all have been born equal, but this refers only to the physical manner we have been conceived and born. That is as far as it goes. Every soul has returned for serving in a different way. Every soul has brought with him completely different backgrounds which could only be looked up in the Akashic records. These rich, full backgrounds explain why geniuses are born every day. They instinctively have brought with them many talents that have taken eons of time to perfect. For these reasons, they have returned at a particular time with those talents. How well they will succeed, depends upon themselves. They can either waste those talents, or can use them to help mankind. Their advancement depends on their use of these talents. Some are regressing, while others are advancing at a rapid rate. God loves all souls, but rejoices at the successes some are making, while others bring only displeasure from the hierarchy. One who wastes his time on this plane brings this displeasure. Yes, you must have a balance of work and rest, but some souls may waste whole lifetimes, not making any attempt to fulfill the goals set before them. Blessed is he that serves the Father with no question as to how or why. Who are you to question your destiny?

Some of you will be saying that you don't know what you were destined to achieved during this life. For this reason, you should learn to look within for those answers. The meditation techniques given in many books in many ways, is a good place to start. You can always look back on your life and find a general trend or pattern evolving before your eyes. You will be able to evaluate your progress from this observation. You can learn to evaluate dreams that tell of your destiny on this plane. Write those dreams down. Learn to interpret them, or have others knowledgeable in dream therapy, interpret them for you. Once you determined what your purpose might be in this life, you must set that plan in motion, if it has not already been done. You must let no man interfere in any way in your being able to carry this plan out to its completion. This is your commitment to the loving Father who has placed you here for a definite purpose.

You may find it difficult at first focusing your attention upon a definite plan, and holding it there. More and more, you will be able to keep your mind focused upon him who has sent you. You will be aware of this creative power and energy flowing through you, serving all mankind. You will cease to seek credit for your accomplishments, but will give full credit where the credit is due, and that is to the Father who has sent you here for a definite purpose.

This is the way you will begin to become humble in the eyes of the Father. This humility is not one which puts you down, so to speak, but one which places you in proper perspective with the Father in heaven. If you can but see that you are but the smallest twig at end of the branches of a tree of life, and the God power comes to you from the base roots of that very tree. Every twig has its own destiny and plan set before him. This should be an exciting challenge for each small twig on that tree. Take up that challenge which has been offered to you, and carry it out to the best of your ability. Sure you will make mistakes, but if you continue to learn from each of those mistakes, you will have advanced rapidly up the path. No failure can be considered such, if you will have learned something from it. These challenges have been set before you, sometimes to see how you will react to each set of circumstances. If you will but learn to meet and master these challenges, you will not have to go back and face them a second time. It is important for you to think out the decisions that you must make in those circumstances, and make the proper decisions. It isn't that you will not have another chance to pass that particular test, because you will have that opportunity many times until you will be able to pass. All is not lost if you fail. Meet the next challenge with renewed vigor, and succeed.

Every challenge which has been met and accomplished successfully, is one more step closer to complete freedom. How fast you will advance up the path is entirely up to you. You must know that the end of that path, you will find the complete freedom for which you so diligently strived. If your goal is in sight, you have deserved this moment. If you never see the end of that path, and you find you are slowly losing sight of that end, you will have deserved that too. Keep your mind steadfastly on that goal, let no man interfere with your progress, and you will move easily along the path. The farther you move up the path, the narrower it becomes. This might seem to be an impossible challenge if you are at the beginning, but as you advance, you will find it is easier to stay on that narrow path than you previously thought. This has been made possible by the dedication you have given to your task before you. The more you advance spiritually, the easier it is to remain dedicated to the plan, and also conversely, you will also find the many temptations set before you as you advance. You will be better equipped to handle the temptations if you have moved higher up on the spiritual ladder. Some of the basic temptations you will encounter at the lower end of the path, may be great hurdles for you to climb over. Therefore your advancement could be quite rapid at the beginning, or very slow, depending on the determination of the soul involved.

You will want to sit down and give thanks for the many challenges set before you, whether they may be good or bad. They need not be either good or bad, but only wonderful opportunities for you to grow and to move along that path to complete freedom. You, as a Westerner, may be asking, "What is this complete freedom?" Jesus came that we might have complete freedom in an instant, if only we would but hold the faith and believe in the truth. Not many souls today have the simple faith it takes to achieve this freedom as rapidly as this. Jesus came that we we might know the truth, and let that truth set us free, yet, two thousand years later we are still involved with many dogmas, and fail to see the simple truth that he brought to us.

We are reaching an era when the return of the Christ will set mankind straight about the simple truth given to us by Jesus. This chapter is being written only to help you see how this can be understood now, and how you might take advantage of this to move up the spiritual ladder. This basic simple truth if set down in its simplest terms is man's understanding of his unity with God. If this is fully understood, there would be no need for the Ten Commandments, nor would there be any need for the myriads of laws man has set forth to insure that he might live as he was meant to. Man's laws become so confusing that they begin to counterdict each other, or they overlap and duplicate each other. We are the smallest of twigs, and we can only bear fruit when we fulfill our destiny on this plane, or any plane. We can advance rapidly on this material plane, much faster than is possible on other levels of existence. We will be advancing on all levels, but only if we so desire to do so. We must all remember that we are not alone as we move along the path. We have many teachers and guides, and many loving souls on all levels, as well as angelic hosts and the son of God and our loving almighty Father; who are all working in our behalf to aid us as we move along. This knowledge alone should make it much easier for you to succeed, as you meet those challenges. You too, will be aiding all those loving hosts who are helping you. Your loving help will insure a rapid spiritual growth for you. You need not make a conscious effort, but it will happen for you if you are living the truth. All are being blessed as you travel.

CHAPTER VIII

HOW DOES THE LAW WORK FOR YOU?

The world law is a confusing term, but one which must be used in this case for clarity. The law referred to in this book always means the law set down according to the the heavenly creator which is the Father of us all. This Universal law is the only true law which we must adhere to. All other laws may be written for our greatest good in mind, but are all limited in scope. Universal Law governs us all equally. We are all bound to the precepts of this law. When we break all man-made laws, we have inadvertedly broken the Universal Law as well. All law conceived by man is inspired by the need to enforce the Universal Law, but many laws have been written to confuse the situation. These laws have been written to help special interest groups, or to bolster the egoes of powerful souls. These laws are evil in concept and are only here to aid the powers of the dark forces. When man breaks these laws, he does not necessarily break the Universal Law given to us by the heavenly Father of us all. You may be thrown in prison for breaking man's laws, but never will you be punished by the hierarchy under God, for not obeying unjust laws. Ask yourself if a law is just or unjust in the eyes of God. You will always have the answer to this if you but ask the Father within for guidance. Man does much to confuse us by the legal phrasing used in preparing these laws. You have teachers and guides who will aid you in making the right decisions in regard to the law. You will be a hero if you obey God's laws and disregard the unjust laws set down by mankind. You must obey all just laws set down by man which have been written to fulfill the tenants of Universal Law.

Jesus has said, "Give to Caesar what is Caesar's, and give to God, what is his". Don't get the idea that all man-made law is unjust, only those laws which have previously been described are the work of the dark forces. When you learn to live and work in the light, you will not need to concern yourself with the unjust laws. You will be guided to make correct decisions and need have no fear of man's inhumanity to man, for those who have broken those unjust laws. Yes Christians today are being tortured and suppressed as they have in the past for their beliefs in God's Universal Law, over cruel, unjust laws set down to take away basic freedoms from man. Those souls who are defending the Universal Laws which govern us all will be moving rapidly along the spiritual path to complete freedom. They have chosen to defend the truth, in a continuing battle with the forces of greed, which has inspired many unjust laws.

We are now going to concentrate on the Universal Law as we know it for the remainder of this chapter. All references to the law from this point on, will refer only to Universal Law as given to us by a loving Father. To be aware of, and to know the Law, is not enough, you must live the law every moment of every day. If all mankind felt this way, there would be no need for man's laws. If you would but realize that there is only one God, and that God is with you, and working through you for the greatest good of all man; you wouldn't have to be concerned about breaking man's laws.

God's law is with us every moment as we travel along the path. We can never escape from the effects of this law, even for a moment. This law permeates all creation. Every stone, plant, and animal is ruled by this law in its own way. Since man has the right to make correct or incorrect decisions, he is set apart from the rest of creation in regard to the law. The lower kingdoms tend to move at a steady pace in their development in regard to the law; whereas, man can move rapidly along the path, or more slowly, or even move backward in his development. Yes, we are definitely in charge of our destiny. We can either respond positively toward the law, or disregard, or twist it out of proportion. The law has been set up to benefit all creation, not just mankind. We often are so concerned with our egoes that we forget about all life about us. How long could we live without the others of the universe flowing through us, feeding and cleansing us with every breath. All the loving energy from other levels are willing to become one with us to sustain us. Our material bodies are compiled solely from the elements of the earth, while our souls are the creation of the Father, which has no beginning and no end.

Our relation with the law determines whether we are to be happy, or sad, rich or poor, healthy or unhealthy, to grow spiritually or to stagnate. More men tend to choose to think negatively about their existence. This creates many problems which must be overcome in accepting the truth about the law. The Christ has shown us the way to be free, and that is to know that you need never go through this trial, but that you only need to know the truth of the Law to be free. Know the truth, and you will inherit the earth. You will be true disciples of the truth. It matters not what others may think of you, but only that you remain in tune with the heavenly Father who hath placed you here for a definite purpose. Many of us are to be teachers of the truth, while others are to be practitioners of the truth. Both are important in the implementation of the law as it has been set up. God has given us the tools to use to help us in abiding within the framework of that law. Strong souls who are working in the truth, will help others see the truth, and live within the framework of the law. We need not try to make converts among others who do not follow the precepts of the law, but that if we but live the truth, it will be known to all men that you are indeed a wise soul who is living the truth. Jesus did not try to impress others with his great knowledge of the law, but he let his light shine forth, spreading the truth before him.

You probably have asked the question, "But what is the Universal Law we have heard so much about"? Oh yes, you have seen it in the Ten Commandments many times, but it is much more than that. You must first recognize your oneness with the Father who has placed you here at this time. This realization must be with you every moment you are awake or asleep on this plane. If this realization is achieved, then you will find it difficult to break the law as it has been set up. If you but realize this fact, you will find it difficult to see the perfection of your fellowman. You will know you are all of one source. How could you lie, cheat, or commit other sins against any other man, when this is fully realized? It would be impossible for you to knowingly or unknowingly, break any of these commandments if this realization is fully understood. You would never again be able to covet any material possessions enjoyed by your brothers. You will fully understand that this is all of the Father, and these are the blessings which he has bestowed upon him. You would definitely forgive all those that would transgress against you. How could you not forgive the Father, when you realize your brother is of the Father, who is supposed to have transgressed against you? Oh and oh, you may go with the concept of the law as you understand it, and you will find that you could not obey the law when you keep the faith, and know and live the truth.

Sure, you will ask, "Why can't mankind find it easier to abide by the law"? When man lets his ego get involved, he leaves himself open for sinning. When man is able to surrender himself completely to the Christ, he will be so filled with ego of the Father, there will be no room for anything else. Once this has taken place, you will have been completely reborn in his name. You will never again go back. Surrender yourself to the Father, and you will be able to go forth with a new understanding of the existence of all creation on this plane. You will not be able to lay waste all that he hath created for your enjoyment, but rather, you will be able to work in harmony with all creation. You will attract all creation which is needed to fulfill your purpose on this plane. Your Father wishes you to enjoy all his many blessings which he has bestowed upon mankind. Only you, and you alone, will try to place limitations upon this natural law of attraction. You have no enemies, you only have the enemies which you have created for your experience.